# FLORIDA
*portrait of a state*

# FLORIDA
*portrait of a state*

GRAPHIC ARTS BOOKS

Library of Congress Control Number: 2006926479
International Standard Book Number: 978-1-55868-989-3

Captions and book compilation © 2007 by
Graphic Arts Books, an imprint of
Graphic Arts Center Publishing Company
P.O. Box 10306, Portland, Oregon 97296-0306
503/226-2402; www.gacpc.com

The five-dot logo is a registered trademark of
Graphic Arts Center Publishing Company.

President: Charles M. Hopkins
Associate Publisher: Douglas A. Pfeiffer
Editorial Staff: Timothy W. Frew, Kathy Howard, Jean Bond-Slaughter
Production Coordinator: Heather Doornink
Cover Design: Elizabeth Watson
Interior Design: Jean Andrews

Printed in China

FRONT COVER: ◗ Miami's South Beach invites sun worshippers year-round.
BACK COVER: ◗ A wood stork, *Mycteria americana,* searches for food in Everglades
National Park. A waterbird standing two to four feet tall, the wood stork weighs up to ten pounds.
◄◄ A starfish graces the beach on Santa Rosa Island, part of Gulf Islands National Seashore.
◄ Bahia Honda State Park, situated in the Florida Keys, has been a destination since 1894.
The Overseas Highway in the background connects the Keys with the mainland.
► Palm, oak, and mixed hardwoods line a river in Hillsborough River State Park.

◄ The lighthouse on Garden Key, in Dry Tortugas
National Park, was originally built in 1825, twenty years before
Florida became a state. In 1877, the original structure was replaced with
the present boilerplate iron tower. The light was deactivated in 1924.
▲ Ginnie Springs, whose waters are a comfortable 72 degrees
year-round, flows out to the Santa Fe River. Scuba
diving is a popular activity at the springs.

◄ Big Talbot Island State Park, on Big Talbot Island off Florida's northeast coast, is a natural preserve utilized for nature study and photography, as well as bird-watching.
▲ The pied-billed grebe, *Podilymbus podiceps,* is seldom seen flying; it prefers to dive rather than flee when danger threatens. Though it swims like a duck, it does not have webbed feet.

◄ The American avocet, *Recurvirostra americana,* is some eighteen inches tall.
▲ LEFT TO RIGHT: ◗ A great egret, *Ardea alba,* watches over two chicks in the nest.
Nestlings can be quite aggressive toward each other, causing a high mortality rate.
◗ Pelicans roost in the trees on Pelican Island, which was established in 1903 as
a federal bird reservation by President Theodore Roosevelt. Members of the
family Pelecanidae, the birds can reach lengths of up to seventy-two inches.

▲ In the Florida Keys, white chairs
and palm trees grace a white-sand beach. The
islands of the Keys change shape constantly, adding sand
on one end while undergoing erosion at the other.

▲ An oceanfront hotel on Miami's South Beach, the
Tides flaunts the classic Art Deco design of L. Murray Dixon.
The Tides Hotel, situated on the site of the first home built on
Miami Beach (1886), was completed in 1936 in the
heart of the picturesque Art Deco district.

▲ The Castillo de San Marcos, constructed from 1672
to 1695, originally served to guard the Spanish community
of St. Augustine, the first permanent European settlement in the
continental United States. It was declared a national monument in 1924.
► A huge Moreton Bay fig tree, *Ficus macrophylla,* flourishes in Selby
Gardens, Sarasota. The tree is quite invasive, often growing
in other trees and eventually replacing its hosts.

◄ Cypress trees line the shores of Lake Eloise.
Cypress trees thrive in water up to their "knees."
▲ In the Ocala National Forest, the Bear Swamp Trail, a
boardwalk trail in the Salt Springs Recreation Area, provides
a glimpse into the ancient forest that once lined the shores of
Salt Springs. The springs gush forth some fifty million gallons
of water daily at a temperature of about 72 degrees.

▲ Dating to the early 1700s, the González-Alvarez
House is the oldest surviving Spanish Colonial dwelling in Florida.
▶ Originally a small homestead, America's oldest wooden schoolhouse
first appeared on St. Augustine's tax rolls in 1716. The schoolmaster lived
upstairs with his family and used the ground floor as a classroom.
Boys and girls were taught in the same classroom, making the
St. Augustine school the first in the nation to go coed.

◄ An American alligator waits for prey.
▲ CLOCKWISE FROM TOP LEFT: ◗ The Shamu
show at SeaWorld Orlando is probably the best known of the
aquatic animal shows at the facility. Others include seals and dolphins.
◗ The eastern tiger salamander, *Ambystoma tigrinum*, is seven to eight inches long.
◗ Manatees, *Trichechus manatus*, swim in the Intracoastal Waterway at
Merritt Island National Wildlife Refuge.

▲ EPCOT, an acronym for Experimental Prototype
Community of Tomorrow, was originally envisioned as a
city of the future from the imagination of Walt Disney. In actuality,
EPCOT became a theme park similar to a world's fair.
▶ Walt Disney World's Magic Kingdom is home to
Cinderella Castle, Splash Mountain, and
numerous other attractions.

◄ In Fort Lauderdale, the Caribbean Mardi
Gras Junior Carnival takes place along Las Olas Boulevard.
Numerous cultural and seasonal festivals add to the mystique that is Florida.
▲ The Asian Cultural Festival in Miami commemorates Admiral Perry's arrival in
Japan in 1853. Perry negotiated treaties that opened up trade between the
United States and Japan. Among the events at the Asian Cultural
Festival is the Hong Kong Dragon Boat Race Festival.

▲ Miami Beach's Art Deco era lasted from
about 1925 to 1945. Since 1976, a festival has taken place
each year to draw attention to the arts and culture of that period.
▶ An Art Deco stairway in Key West demonstrates the interior
beauty so prevalent in the Art Deco Historic District.

▲ The roseate spoonbill, *Ajaia ajaja,*
inhabits marshes, tidal ponds, sloughs,
and mangrove swamps along the Gulf Coast.
► Silhouetted against a setting sun, cattails
line the shore of Lake Hamilton.

◄ Lily pads adorn a pond in Jonathan Dickinson State Park.
▲ Blowing Rocks Preserve is a barrier island sanctuary on Jupiter
Island. The name comes from the fact that during high
seas, waves break against the rocks, forcing plumes
of saltwater up to fifty feet skyward.

▲ Spider lily, *Hymenocallis crassifolia,* blooms
in Loxahatchee National Wildlife Refuge. The plant,
which reaches from eighteen inches to four feet tall,
flourishes in up to six inches of standing water.

▲ At Butterfly World near Fort Lauderdale,
a *Heliconius* butterfly (family Heliconiidae) rests
for a moment on a Mexican sunflower
(*Tithonia rotundifolia*).

▲ A row of stately Cuban royal palms, *Roystonea regia,* and
bougainvilleas form a wall in Miami. The Cuban royal palm was
imported from around Havana, Cuba, into Florida in the 1920s and 1930s.
▶ The waterways, homes, and yachts of the Miami waterfront are
backdropped by the high-rises of downtown.

◄ A sailboat enters Key West's Old Town Harbor at sunset.
▲ The Jacksonville skyline glows through the spraying water from the
Friendship Fountain. Constructed in 1965, the fountain was touted
as the world's largest and tallest, shooting as high as 120 feet.

▲ A charming 110-mile highway running the length of the Keys,
the Overseas Highway connects Key West to the Florida mainland.
▶ Sabal palms, *Sabal palmetto*, rise above a coreopsis-carpeted meadow in
Myakka River State Park, one of Florida's oldest and largest state parks.

◄ Outlined against early morning fog near Venice, Spanish
moss, *Tillandsia usneoides,* drapes a pine tree, adding a ghostly look.
▲ Kumquat is a sweet-and-sour fruit, a member of the citrus
family. Most kumquats in the United States are
grown in the area around Saint Joseph.

▲ On Florida beaches, one can be as active,
or inactive, as one chooses. Sailing, searching for shells
along the beach, sunbathing—or enjoying a nap
in a hammock are among the choices.

▲ CLOCKWISE FROM TOP LEFT: Other pursuits include—
● Playing a sand game of volleyball, this one on Clearwater Beach;
● Watching a newborn paint filly with her mother on a horse breeding farm;
● Fishing, as a child shows his mother his catch on the Indian River;
● Or enjoying an airboat excursion into the Florida Everglades.

▲ A hybrid orchid lends its delicate
color to Selby Gardens, in Sarasota. The
Orchidacae family is earth's most rapidly changing
group of plants, with more than 28,000 species.
▶ Palm trees silhouetted against a sunset sky rise
above Clearwater Beach, on the Gulf Coast.

▲ Near Immokalee, indigo buntings,
*Passerina cyanea,* seem to be having a serious
discussion. The indigo bunting is a good neighbor
to farmers and fruit growers, consuming
many insect pests and weed seeds.

▲ Mangroves, genus *Rhizophora,* flourish
in the Florida Everglades. They generally grow in
areas greatly influenced by the daily tides but
protected from excessive wave action.

▲ Cypress Gardens, near Winter Haven, opened in 1936
as a showplace for eight thousand varieties of flowers from more than
ninety countries. Closed in 2003 because of declining attendance, it was
reopened in 2004 as Cypress Gardens Adventure Park. It now features
concerts, a water park, animal exhibits, carnival rides, and
water ski shows, in addition to the traditional gardens.

▲ *Gaillardia pulchella* covers the ground
with brilliant color, ranging from rose-purple
in the centers to yellow, orange, crimson, or copper
scarlet on the outer petals. Common names are
blanket flower, firewheel, and Indian blanket.

▲ The Ocala National Forest provides
recreational opportunities along a seven-mile
canoe trail in Alexander Springs Creek.

▲ A purple gallinule, *Porphyrula martinica*, forages
among lily pads in Everglades National Park. Their size
(10.5 inches long with a wingspan of 21 inches), blue plumage,
and fearsome bill make them easy birds to identify.

▲ Cattails line a pond at the Royal Palm Visitor Center in Everglades National
Park. Offerings at the visitor center include several hiking and biking trails, as well as access
to the Anhinga Trail boardwalk, where alligators are often seen congregating in watering holes.

▶ Wandering Jew mixes with crown of thorns flowers. Wandering Jew is one of several
creeping plants of the genus *Tradescantia*, in the spiderwort family. Crown of thorns,
*Euphorbia milii*, gets its common name from a legend that says it was the
plant used to create the crown Jesus wore at the crucifixion.

52

◄ A belted kingfisher, *Ceryle alcyon,*
watches along waterways to catch small fish.
▲ In Bonita Springs, the Hyatt Regency Coconut
Point Resort and Spa welcomes corporate clients. The
Raptor Bay Golf Course is only one of the many attractions.
►► A beach ball caught in grass bears mute testimony to the myriad
activities enjoyed in a state edged on three sides by beach.

◄ A diver investigates a turtle swimming above
a coral reef, one of some six thousand reefs found between
Key Biscayne and Dry Tortugas. Both turtles and tortoises are reptiles;
turtles spend their time in water, while tortoises are land animals.
▲ In Key Largo, schoolmaster snappers school together. Some
80 percent of fish school at some point in their lives, forming
groups ranging from six or eight to thousands.

▲ A couple on jet skis races past upscale homes on Palm Island.

► Known as T. Y. Park for short, the Seminole name of this 150-acre park, *Topeekeegee Yugnee,* means "meeting or gathering place." Among numerous activities offered is a water playground complex.

◄ CLOCKWISE FROM TOP LEFT: Florida is home to a wide variety of birds:
• Barn owls in the downy stage, sharing a nesting box on a sugarcane farm;
• A whooping crane and her chick, part of a nonmigratory flock in Kissimmee Prairie;
• A female anhinga, also called a snakebird, appearing to laugh at the world; and
• A wood duck and her ducklings at Edward Ball Wakulla Springs State Park.
▲ Near Bushnell, a red fox, *Vulpes vulpes*, watches over her kit near their den.

▲ Sailboats dock at a marina at Mallory Square in Key
West, in the Florida Keys. The Keys are a favorite area for sailing.
▶ The Rocks Beach edges Washington Oaks Gardens, famous not only
for its formal gardens that feature both native and exotic plants but also
for the unique coquina rock formations that line its Atlantic beach.

◄ In 1921, Edward W. Bok contracted with
Frederick Law Olmsted Jr. to create a lush, subtropical
garden. Then, in 1927, Bok commissioned Milton B. Medary
to design and build a carillon tower to reign over the gardens.
Bok Tower, made of Georgia marble, was finished in 1929.
▲ Indian Shores Beach, in the Clearwater area,
lies along Florida's upper Gulf Coast.

▲ Christy Payne Mansion, now utilized as a
museum in Sarasota's Selby Gardens, is a unique
example of eclectic Southern Colonial architecture.
▶ A three-inch miniature pineapple (inedible)
embellishes the Naples Botanical Garden.

◄ Catamarans accent the Florida Keys. A catamaran is a vessel,
often a sailboat, with twin hulls; a deck usually connects the two.
▲ The courtyard of the Ringling Museum of Art shows the beauty of some of
the sixty-six-acre Ringling Estate on Sarasota Bay. The John and Mable Ringling
Museum of Art was established in 1927 as the legacy of John Ringling and his wife, Mable.
►► Architectural details of Cà d'Zan Mansion in Sarasota Bay show its brick and terra cotta
construction. The elaborate home of John and Mable Ringling was completed in 1926.

▲ Fort Lauderdale marinas offer boat slips,
maintenance, and services to all kinds of oceangoing
craft—boats, yachts, and megayachts—that dock in the marinas.
▶ The Hemingway House, situated in Key West, was home to legendary
author Ernest Hemingway for more than ten years. This is where
he wrote *To Have and Have Not,* which is set in Key West.

◄ Sanibel Island is a barrier island just off Florida's southwest
coast, near Fort Myers. A mere twelve miles long and four miles
wide, the island is a much sought-after place for shell hunting.
▲ The white ibis, *Eudocimus albus,* is a medium-sized wading
bird, averaging about twenty-five inches long, with
a wingspan of up to thirty-eight inches.

▲ Seagulls soar along a windswept
beach at Dr. Julian G. Bruce St. George Island
State Park. The park has nine miles of undeveloped
beaches and dunes, surrounded by the emerald waters of the
Gulf of Mexico. Recreational opportunities include fishing,
shelling, bird-watching, swimming, canoeing, boating,
hiking, camping, and nature study.

▲ Wild columbine, *Aquilegia canadensis*,
reaches heights of two to three feet. The flowers are
pollinated by hummingbirds, which depend on wild
columbine as an important source of nectar.

▲ Construction on Fort Jefferson, on Garden Key in the
Dry Tortugas, began in 1846 just a year after Florida became a state.
The fort was never completed, but in 1935 the area was designated as Fort Jefferson
National Monument. It was changed to Dry Tortugas National Park in 1992.

▶ At Lake Woodruff National Wildlife Refuge, arrowroot plants *(Maranta
arundinacea)* thrive among the grasses bordering freshwater ponds.

◄ Completed in 1887, the Ponce de Leon Inlet
Light Station, twelve miles south of Daytona Beach, is
Florida's tallest lighthouse, towering 175 feet above the waves.
▲ A bird's-eye view of the Everglades and Florida Bay gives little hint
of the complex ecosystem of the Glades. Containing both temperate and
tropical plant communities, the Everglades are home to rich bird life,
mammals, and reptiles—including both alligators and crocodiles.

▲ A forest of bamboo, *Phyllostachys atrovaginata,*
graces Selby Gardens in Sarasota. Bamboo, actually a
grass, ranges in size from a few inches tall to giant
timbers more than one hundred feet in height.

▲ Yellow blossoms of squash plants brighten
a field near Homestead. Though most people think
of Florida as a vacation destination, agriculture utilizes
some ten million acres of the land. In 2000, Florida ranked
ninth in the nation in cash receipts from agriculture.

▲ Bogie Channel, on No Name Key,
is a great place for kayaking among the mangroves.
▶ A lady's slipper orchid, *Paphiopedilum* spp., adorns Selby Gardens.
▶▶ A beach chair and umbrella beckon on South Beach Miami.

◄ The Basilica Cathedral of St. Augustine has the oldest written parish records in the nation, dating from 1594. Located on the Plaza de la Constitución, the Cathedral incorporates the 1797 parish church and is one of the oldest Catholic religious buildings in the United States.

▲ The spiral staircase inside the St. Augustine Lighthouse echoes the distinctive black-and-white spiral design of the exterior. In 1824 St. Augustine became the site of the first lighthouse established in Florida by the new territorial American government.

▲ Clockwise from left: Florida's wildlife includes—
◗ The Florida panther, *Puma concolor coryi*, one of more than
twenty subspecies of cougar, the official state animal of Florida;
◗ The key deer, *Odocoileus virginianus clavium*, the smallest of all white-
tailed deer, reaching only twenty-four to twenty-eight inches tall; and
◗ Wild boar, *Sus scrofa*, with an average life span of about ten years.
▶ A snowy egret, *Egretta thula*, waits for dinner to swim by.

◄ Nine Mile Pond in Everglades National Park
provides a calm look—but take care! That's not a log
in the water; an alligator lies in wait in the peaceful-looking pond.
▲ Cocoa Beach, situated on a barrier island between the Atlantic Ocean and
the Banana River Lagoon on Florida's central east coast, is just six miles long
and less than a mile wide. Cocoa Beach is popular with surfboarders.

▲ The sun sets over Apalachee Bay in Saint Marks National Wildlife Refuge. The refuge was established in 1931 to provide wintering habitat for migratory birds. Encompassing 68,000 acres along the Gulf Coast of northwest Florida, it is one of the oldest refuges in the National Wildlife Refuge System.

▲ Black-eyed Susans, *Rudbeckia hirta*, flourish just about
anywhere—in open woods, gardens, fields, and along roadsides.
They tend to take over an area, pushing other plants out.

C<small>LOCKWISE FROM TOP LEFT</small>: Florida's wetlands provide habitat for frogs—
⬩ The Brazilian horned frog, *Ceratophrys cranwelli*, uses its huge mouth to gulp up
prey, including insects, other frogs, and mice. It can swallow prey almost as large as itself;
⬩ The barking tree frog, *Hyla gratiosa*, gets its common name because the male "barks" during rain; and
⬩ The squirrel treefrog, *Hyla squirella*, makes a grating sound like a squirrel: hence, its common name.
▶ A painted lady butterfly, *Vanessa cardui*, rests on a purple coneflower, *Echinacea purpurea*.
The painted lady is found on every continent except Antarctica.

▲ A red passion flower, *Passiflora coccinea*,
flourishes in Sarasota's Selby Botanical Gardens.
▶ Shell Key, in Everglades National Park, has been
shaped by hurricanes, waves, and changing tides
for some 3,000 years. It is a destination for
snorkeling, birding, and watching the
dolphins that cavort in the area.

◄ *Dropped Bowl with Scattered Slices and Peels,*
by Claes Oldenburg and Coosje van Bruggen, is a huge
outdoor sculpture with multidimensional sections. It represents
orange slices and peels in a bowl shattered on the ground.
▲ Watson Island, located at the western end of Miami
Harbor, is connected to Miami proper
via the MacArthur Causeway.

103

▲ The underwater *Christ Statue,* designed by
Italian sculptor Guido Galletti, sits atop a concrete base
in twenty-five feet of water in Key Largo Marine Sanctuary.
It is the site of some two hundred underwater weddings each year.

▶ A couple dives among elkhorn coral, *Acropora palmata,* in Looe
Key. Elkhorn coral was listed as a threatened species in 2006.

◄ Situated in front of the Jackie Gleason
Theater of the Performing Arts, the *Mermaid* sculpture,
designed by Roy Lichtenstein, captures the spirit of Miami Beach.
▲ The John D. MacArthur Beach State Park protects 438
acres. In the 1970s, MacArthur donated the land
to preserve the subtropical coastal habitat.

▲ Miami at dusk is an unforgettable sight.
High-rises and city lights reflecting along the waterfront
lend a romantic look to the city. Miami-Dade County
has a population of more than 2,250,000.

▲ Jacksonville presents a brilliant skyline at night.
► In Miami, Fourth of July fireworks light up sky and water.
►► Nine Mile Pond, in Everglades National Park, sees a double sunset—
one in the sky, and the other reflected in the water beneath.
Water trails, used by kayakers and canoers, are available
year-round except when water levels run too low.